AF380619

Ready for your first horse?

Cheat Sheet Summaries of the very basics in Horse Care, Riding and Owning a Horse

Debbie Burgermeister

Copyright © 2019

The moral right of Debbie Burgermeister to be identified as the author
and Meftahul Amin to be identified as the cover illustrator
has been asserted by them in accordance with the Copyright, Design and
Patents Act 1988.

All rights reserved. No part of this book may be reproduced or
transmitted in any form or by any means, electronic or mechanical,
including photocopying, recording, or by any information storage and
retrieval system, without permission in writing from the copyright owner,
except for the inclusion of brief quotations in a review.

A catalogue record for this
book is available from the
National Library of Australia

ISBN: 9781981812547

Book creation, editing, design and layout by Crazy Diamond Publishing
Print and channel distribution: Lightning Source / Ingram
Publisher: Horse Riding Hub

www.horseridinghub.com

DISCLAIMER: "All content, including text, graphics, images and
information, contained on or available through this book is for general
information purposes only. Such information is subject to change without
notice. You are encouraged to confirm any information obtained from or
through this book with other sources and professionals."

Experience the love, passion, energy and freedom of horses!

Your author Debbie has a lifetime of horsemanship experience, in-depth knowledge to share, and a passion for people of all ages learning safely. She is committed to helping people who are just starting out with the core fundamentals to become sensible, confident, and capable horse handlers and riders.

We hope you enjoy these summaries from an expert who has owned, cared for and loved her horses through many ups and downs. These cheat sheets will set you on a good start to your horse pathway.

RIDE, RELAX, ENJOY!

Cheat Sheet Summaries

Need to know basics

1. How to handle a horse

- The approach, behaviour signs, pack behaviour
- Catching with a halter in a paddock and stable
- Feed time
- Tying knots
- Leading
- Control and respect training
- Rugging

2. Grooming

- Brush types
- Hoof cleaning
- After work sponge or hose, scraper, towel dry, drying rug
- Clipping

3. Saddling

- Saddle types
- Saddle cloths
- Girth types

4. Bridles and bits

- Bridle types
- Bit types
- Putting on a horse

5. Riding and training skills

- Halt, Walk, Trot, Canter, Gallop
- English vs Western riding
- Learning stages and key tasks for safe management of a horse
- Riding environments experience in arena, open area, road, bush, creek
- Group riding in arena and trail
- Training for disciplines
- Behaviour management when frisky, lethargic, lunging, other techniques for raring, pigrooting, bucking, shying

6. Rider gear

- Jodhpurs or jeans
- Boots with a heel
- Safety Helmet AS/NZS 3838, European standard VG1
- Shirt / Safety vest
- Gloves
- Crop/Spurs

Horse safety tips

Horses are great to be around, following the safety rules.

Horses frighten easily. There are simple rules to avoid danger around horses:

- always WALK, never run
- avoid loud and sudden noises

Horses display anger or show they are scared when:

- their ears go back
- they show the white part of their eye

Never walk too close to horses' back legs as they are big animals and can injure you if they kick.

To avoid startling your horse, talk when approaching and always approach calmly towards the shoulder, the safe zone.

Be careful and safe, confident and positive. Horses can sense your feelings and try their best to help you.

Be firm and kind to your horse. They will respond with trust and willingness.

Wear a helmet when riding.

Wear boots around horses and when riding.

Learning pathway
Horse care and handling

- Horse Intro and Fundamentals of Horse Care.

- Handling horses safely and confidently

- Riding Balance preparation skills.

FOUNDATION

Safety tips and horse sense

Communication

Hold and lead with confidence

LEVEL 1

Grooming kit usage and front feet pick up

Mount and dismount

Rider ground exercises

LEVEL 2

Halter, catch and tie with quick release knot

Horse parts

Measure and weigh a horse

Saddlery

LEVEL 3

Gender, colours, markings and breeds

Rugging

Hoof Care

Saddle Up

LEVEL 4

Worming (calculated) and shoeing frequency/hoof care

Bandaging for jumping/first aid

Bridle

Balanced Rider

LEVEL 5

Feeding, managing a horse in paddock, body weight score, read a brand

Rein Control and leg aids

Understand different bits and saddles / how to pull apart gear

Grooming care after riding, how to pull off a shoe

First aid treatments (colic, rainscald, wounds, antibiotics)

Floating and towing

Learning pathway

Horse riding skills

Personalised, achievement focused with a full horse experience.

FOUNDATION

Ground exercise

Mount and dismount

Correct riding position – balance, stand in stirrup

Emergency controls

Rein control at halt

Walk, stop, turn controls

LEVEL 1 - Beginners

Gear check

Mount and dismount drill

Mounted exercises

Rein control at walk

Transitions walk/halt/walk

Rider Aids

Arena circle patterns 10/20m/figure eight

LEVEL 2 - Trotters

Mounted exercises at walk

Arena patterns serpentine and rein changes

Transitions walk/trot/walk

Rein control at trot

Sit trot and rise trot, correct diagonal

Hand technique and leg aids

LEVEL 3 - Canters

Correct trot diagonal, balanced horse and rider

Sit trot serpentines

Shorten and lengthen stride at trot

Canter basics

Intro to different disciplines jump poles, sporting, dressage

Inside and outside leg aid control

LEVEL 4 - Advanced

Trail ride

Leg yield side pass, turns forehand and hind, backup

Flexing around circles

Transitions between walk to trot to canter to walk

Figure eight canter trot and walk changes / canter hand gallop

Bareback to trot

Dressage test

Jumping to 30cm

LEVEL 5 – Advanced 2 Horsemanship

Lunging walk/trot/canter (roller, side reins), square stand

Canter on request from any gait, complex changes

Leg yield spins, side pass, back up and adapt to discipline

One handed riding walk/trot/canter and open gate

Horse training and head carriage (running rein, double rein)

Riding with speed control collected and extended

Bareback to canter

Jump to 60cm (cross, double, course)

Natural Horsemanship, connection/energy work

Horse parts

Parts of the body – Horse head

Say hello to Casanova.

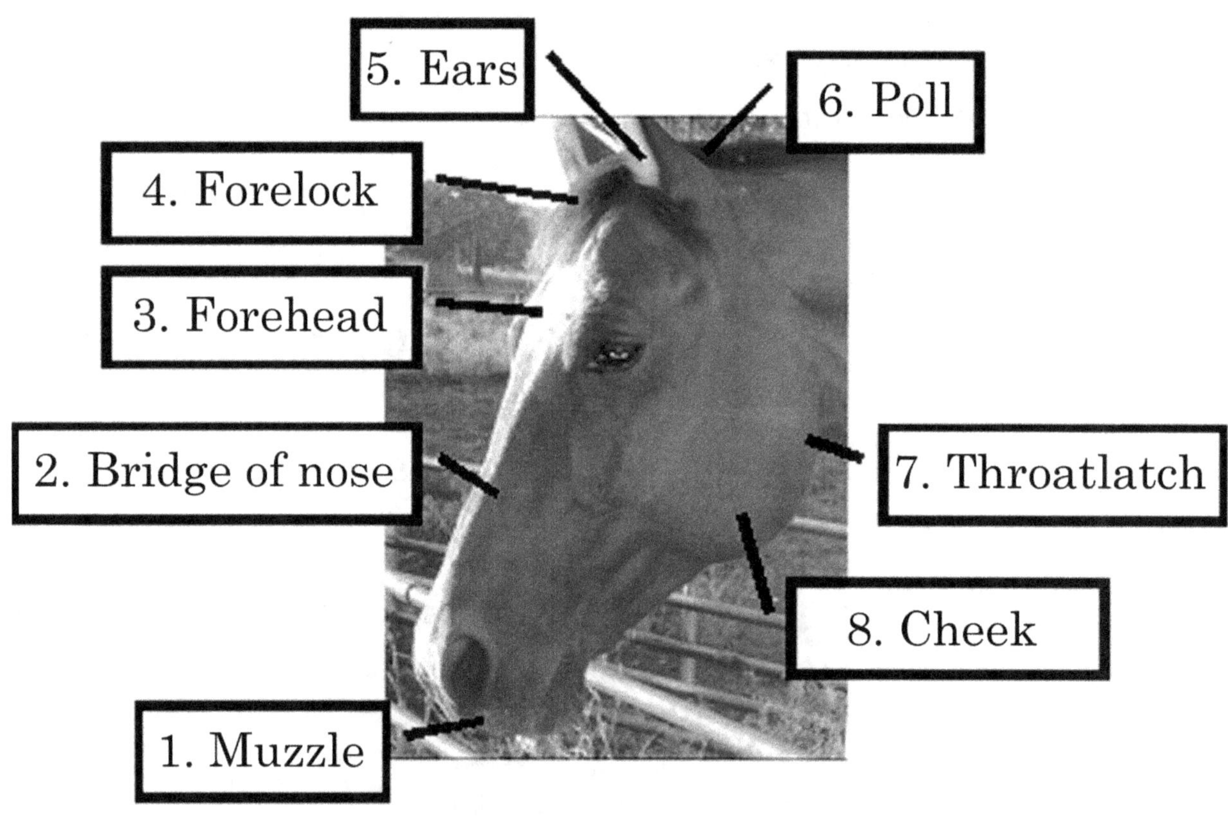

Parts of the body - Horse neck to rear

Say hello to Asha.

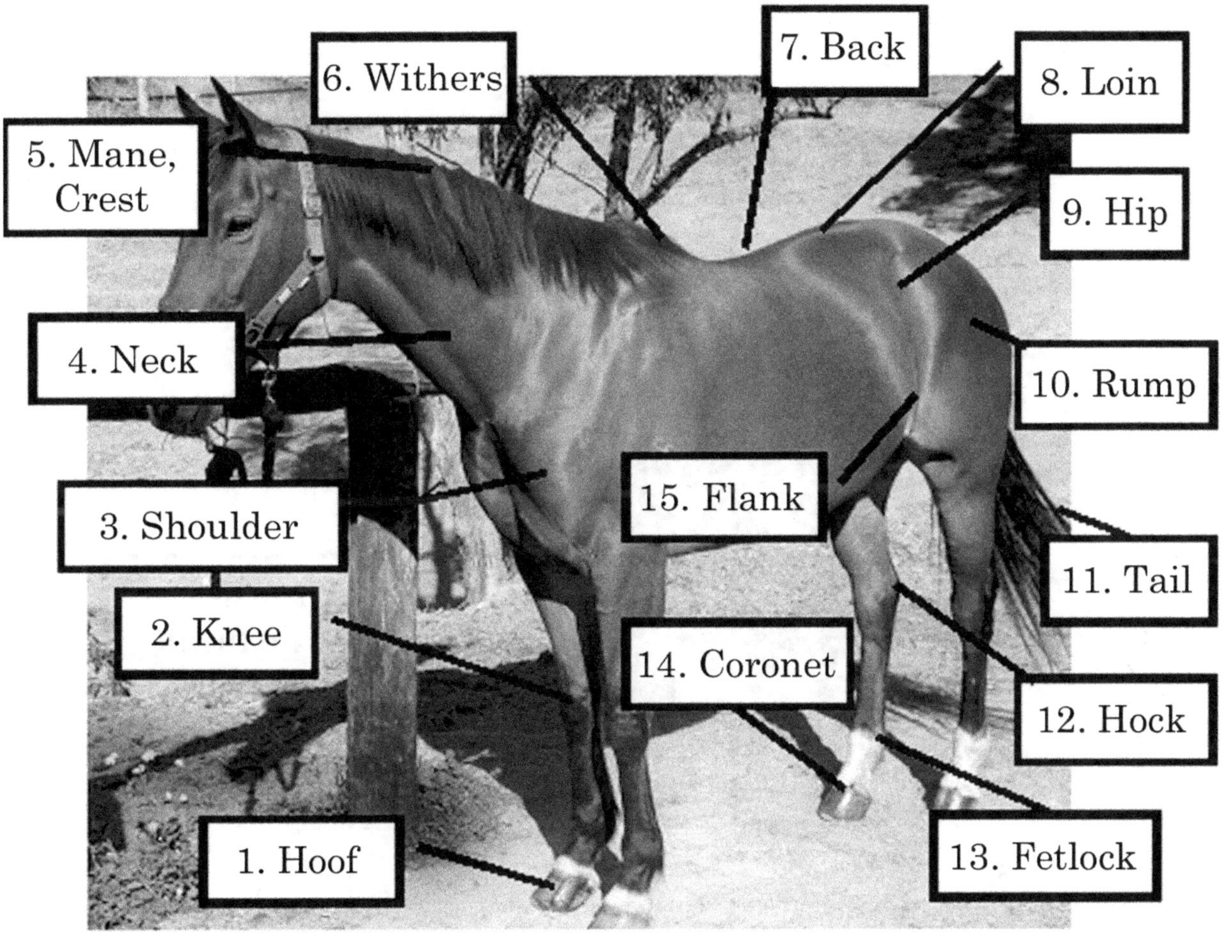

Saddlery parts
The halter and bridle

Say hello to Magic.

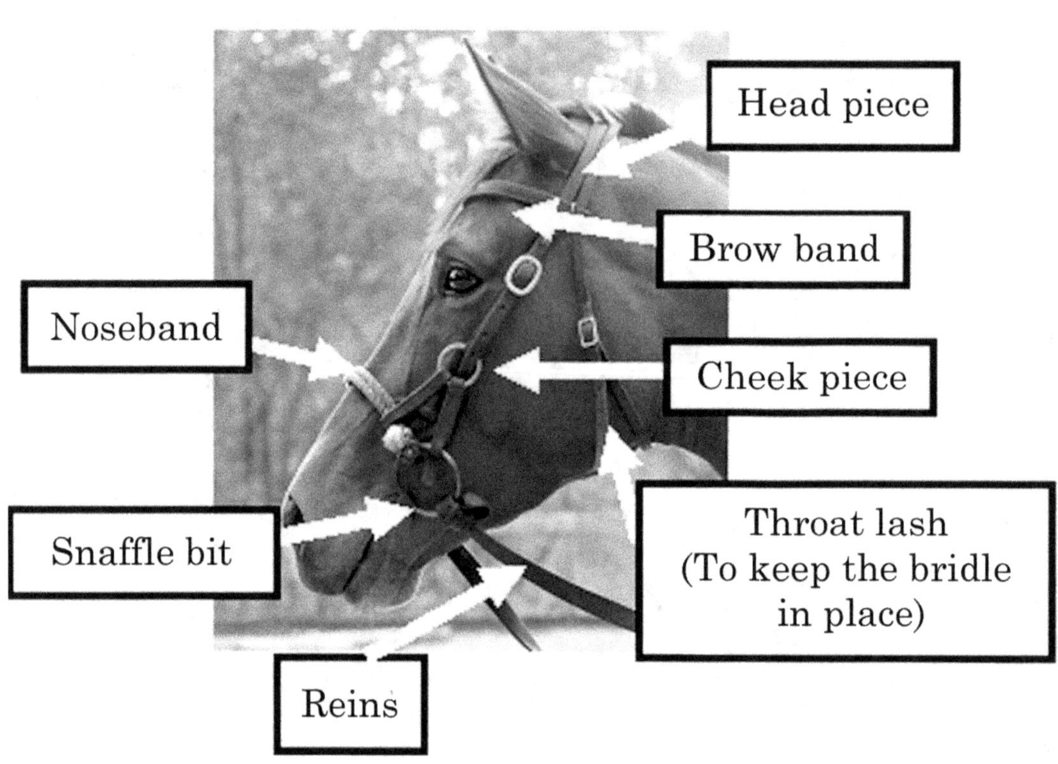

The saddle

Pommel
Waist
Seat
Cantle
Skirt
Lining
Saddle flap
Surcingle loop
Stirrup leather
Stirrup iron

Lining
Cantle
Saddle flap
Sweat flap
Gullet
Girth straps

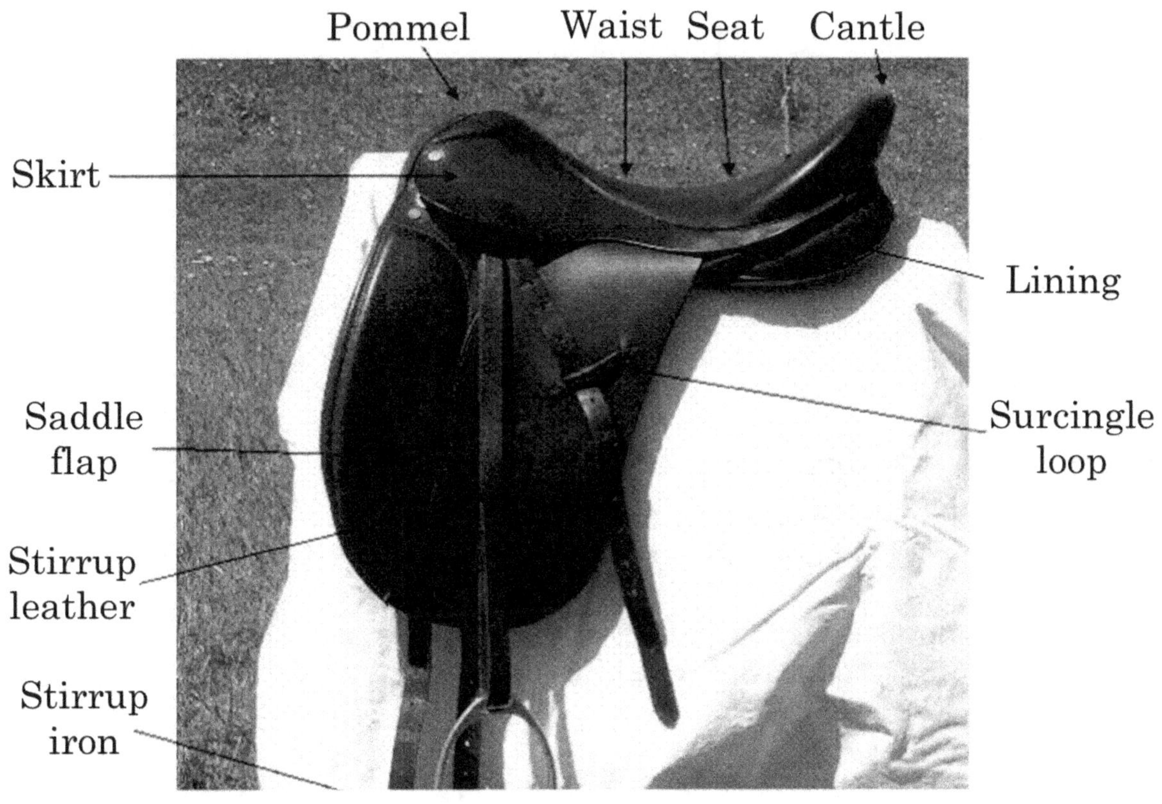

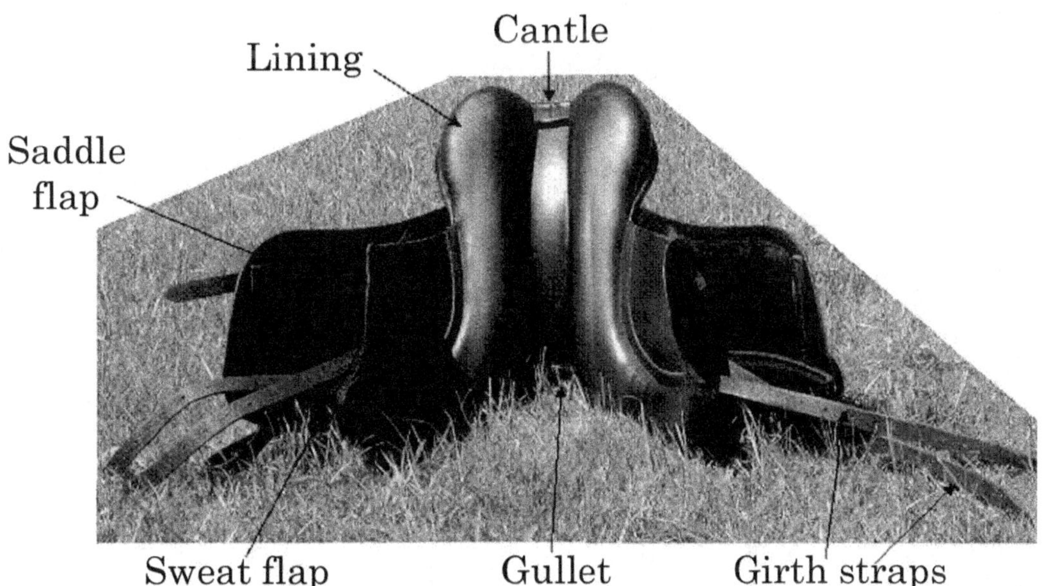

Feeding and nutrition

1. Body Score Index

- Horse age (old signs)
- Weight
- Belly
- Neck
- Rump
- Back

2. Exercise and Performance assessment feeding

- In spelling (no work/at rest)
- Light work (example diet: pellets/barley and chaff plus hay)
- Moderate
- Hard / high energy / high fitness performance objectives
- Fattening feeds (barley, rice bran, pollard)
- Energy (oats, corn, lupins)

3. Behaviours

- Flighty / nervous (B12, Thiamine)
- Fizzy
- Sour

4. Paddock grazing / roughage volume

- Amount of grass
- Quality of grass / protein
- Chaff type (white, lucerne)
- Hay type (lucerne, haylage, rhodes, grassy, barley)

5. Vitamins and Supplements

- Salt and mineral blocks
- Molasses (coat condition, feed palatability)
- Oils (canola for arthritis/aged horses, rice bran for fattening)
- Bi Carb soda (for horses prone to colic or tying up)
- Yoghurt (good for runny tummy)
- Calcium / Lime (in deficient areas)
- Garlic, Sulphur, Herbs, Sunflower seeds (immunity, coat condition, keep bugs away, darken coat)
- Colloidal silver (immunity)
- Joint supplement (arthritis/aged horses)
- Stem Cell Nutrition – StemEquine* (arthritis/laminitis/respiratory/ lameness)

(https://bvhr.stemtech.com/)

First aid and health care

1. Common occurrences

- Bots
- Dry hoof
- Seedy toe
- Greasy heel
- Rain scald / Mud fever
- Girth gall
- Colds (runny nose, cough)
- Tying up (acidic, too much grain and not enough work)
- Queensland itch
- Elbow scabs
- Ticks
- Cuts and grazes

2. Less common

- Ringworm
- Strangles
- Tetanus
- Hendra virus
- Founder / Laminitis
- Colic
- Rat bait poison

3. Bandaging

- Wounds
- Sport
- Bellboots
- Travelling

4. Regular care

- Shoeing/Trimming
- Worming
- Dentist
- Chiro / Massage / Acupuncture
- Vaccinations

5. Sample First Aid Kit

- Gauze wipes / Cotton wool / Jelnet
- Bandages (vetflex and vetwrap)
- Kelato Gel / Prednoderm
- Terrimycn powder / Eye ointment
- Ice pack / boots
- Scissors / Bot knife / Razor blade
- Kerosene
- Iodine / Vetadine wash / Betadine
- White ointment / Zinc / Vaseline / Sea minerals ointment
- Domoso / Bute
- Poultice / Swelldown / Hoof boot / Epsom Salts
- Magnetic boots/rug
- Itch wash (1 part methylated spirits to 2 parts vinegar)
- Sea minerals spray / iodine spray / peroxide and water spray
- Harlem oil / Stockholm tar
- Bicarbonate of soda
- Fly spray (baby oil, apple cider vinegar, lavender oil, eucalyptus oil, dish washing liquid)
- Cetrigen (purple spray)

Grooming kit essentials

1. Reasons for grooming a horse:

- To clean the horse, remove mud, sweat and old hair
- To notice any irregularities and injuries
- To stimulate blood flow to the skin for a healthier coat and muscle tone
- To improve overall appearance – healthy and shiny
- To bond with the horse

2. Basic necessities:

- Hoof pick
- Dandy brush – slightly harder for removing mud
- Curry comb – for removing mud and old hair and stimulates blood flow
- Body brush – slightly softer for all over to remove dust
- Sponges
- Mane comb
- Water brush
- Sweat scraper
- Small plastic bucket

3. Extras:

- Hoof oil and brush
- Bot knife
- Scissors
- Plait bands and tape
- Vaseline
- Hoof black-it for competitions

Owning a horse

1. Owning options

- Buy a horse (price based on age, education and vices)
- Lease
- Hire as you go
- Borrow

2. What do you want?

- Colour
- Breed
- Age
- Height
- Temperament (bombproof, energetic, calm/easy going, no vices)
- Conformation (body type, perfection, blemishes and scars)
- Perfection (blemishes and scars, markings)
- Education and training

3. Adverts and Viewing

- A lot can be worked out from advert wording
- Ask for a video
- See and ride
- Understanding terms in ads
- Vet check / Self assessment
- Riding experience stated
- Catching, tying, handling, grooming, saddle and bridle
- Compare

4.Costs of owning a horse per week (minimum $250AUD/wk)

Horses are expensive to keep with many uncontrollable factors, and this is after the initial purchase price averaging from $2000-$4000 to $20,000 onwards. There is no such thing as a free horse. Basic minimum costs, excluding land rates, utilities, building fences/shelters, and float/truck purchase, are:

- Travel needed (horse float, truck) hire or own maintenance/extra fuel $50/wk
- Own property/agistment self care $50/wk
- Set up of gear and saddlery maintenance (halter, rugs, saddle, bridle, saddlecloth, feeders, grooming, first aid, riding attire, jodhpurs, boots, helmet, whip, spurs) $40/wk
- Feed: Hay for roughage $25/wk
- Feed: Grain for weight or energy $25/wk
- Feed: Chaff for roughage $10/wk
- Feed: Supplements for minerals, electrolytes, joints, behaviour $20/wk
- Dentistry/Vaccinations (tetanus, influenza, hendra) once a year $8/wk
- Deworming every 2-3 months $2/wk
- Farrier shoeing every six weeks (minimal for trim only) $20/wk
- Optional: Riding development: casual, enjoyment, improvement, lessons
- Optional: Insurances
- Optional: Competition entry, associations, travel to events
- Optional: Horse breeding and managing a foal
- Uncontrollable: feed increase due to drought or bad weather
- Uncontrollable: something that can really throw your budget is unexpected veterinarian bills. The cost for out of hours calls can be very expensive, colic treatment or surgery can cost thousands. Having vet cover and mortality insurance can help handle these situations.

5. Fencing and facilities

- Heights and spacing for fences and stables
- Wire and post
- Electric fencing
- Post and rail

About your horse

Your horse and you – Things to know

Horse Name: __________

Father (Sire): __________

Mother (Dam): __________

Microchip: __________

Height: __________

Measured in hands (hh), each hand is 4 inches (10cm) and taken horizontal from the withers. E.g. 100cm(1m) = 10hh.

As a guide ponies are up to 14hh, Galloway is 14-15hh, Hack or Horse is over 15hh.

Weight: __________

Can be measured with a special measure tape. Ponies 200-360kg, Horses 350-600kg, Heavy Horse 550-800kg.

Age: ___________

(foal under 1 getting milk from mum, weanling under 1 no longer getting milk from mum, yearling 1-2yrs, filly and colt 2-3yrs, horse from 4yrs+).

Gender: ___________

(Filly and colt under 4yrs, mare, gelding, stallion 4+)

Breed: ___________

Andalusian, Appaloosa, Australian Stock Horse (ASH), Australian Riding Pony, Arab, Brumby, Clydesdale or Draught, Friesian, Holsteiner, Lipizzaner, Miniature, Quarter Horse (QH), Paint or Pinto, Palomino, Piebald or Skewbald, Shetland, Standardbred, Thoroughbred, Waler, Warmblood, Welsh Pony.

Registration: ___________

Brand: ___________

Usually two sets of numbers indicating the number of the foal and the birth year. Letters or symbols refer to the breeder or society.
For instance: **14**

5

This means it is the fourteenth foal born in 2005 or 2015 on that property/ stud. Usually the horse will show its age sufficiently to tell us which decade it would be.

Markings: _____________

You will generally see white points on a horse and they all have different terms such as:

LEGS: Coronet (small white line above hoof), Half Pastern (wide white marking above hoof), Sock (as it sounds), Stocking (like a long white sock from hoof to knee)

FACE: Star (between eyes), Blaze (between eyes to end of nose), Snip (white between nostrils), Bald (most front of face white), Stripe (thin white blaze like a line from eyes to nose)

Colour: _____________

Good Reference: *http://www.equusite.com/articles/basics/basicsColors.shtml*

The basic colours you will see are Brown, Bay (brown with black mane and tail and usually a black strip on top of rump to tail), Black, Chestnut (red/ orange with mane and tail same colour as coat), Flaxen is with a lighter mane and tail, Liver Chestnut is a very dark chestnut, White or Light grey and they are born white (variations from dapple grey to flea bitten with black sprinkled through the coat).

Other colours can be mixed with the name of a breed as well such as Cremellos (white mane and tail with pink skin), Roan (reddish and blue mix of colours with white), Palomino (golden with white mane and tail), Paint/Pinto (black and white is piebald and brown and white is skewbald), Appaloosa (looks like a leopard white with dark spots)

Horse Healthcare Checklist

Horse name: __________

Last drench: __________

(worming approx. every 8-12weeks)

Last shoeing: __________

(approx. every 5-8weeks)

Last tetanus/strangles vaccination (equivac 2in1): __________

(yearly)

Teeth: __________

(yearly)

Body work: __________

(chiropractor / acupuncture as needed)

Last Hendra vaccination __________

(yearly)

Selling a horse

1. Decision to sell

- Outgrown
- Behaviour / Danger
- Performance / Education level
- Quality / Conformation
- Competition / Discipline focus

2. Preparation to sell

- Grooming
- Rugging
- Riding / Training
- Handling (groundwork, catching, feet, clippers, loading, tying)

3. Advertising

- Newspaper (horse deals, trading post, local newspaper)
- Websites (horsedeals, petlink, gumtree, horseyard, trading post, business website, facebook horse sale sites)
- Local community boards
- Wording
- Pictures / Video

4. Buyers

- Phone calls
- Emails
- Site unseen / Viewings
- Inclusions
- Transport

5. Payment and arrangements

- Trial/lease requests (not recommended)
- Payment options
- Pickup / Delivery
- Written Sale agreement (request a copy example if you need one by email to *info@horseridinghub.com.au*).

Competing

or just for fun

1. Discipline choice

- Options (pleasure, dressage, showing, eventing, pony club, interschool, campdrafting/team penning/cutting/reining, showing, jumping, polo, polocrosse, tricks/liberty, breaking and training)
- Interest and passion
- Fees
- Horse skill
- Cost of horse
- Transport and travel
- Uniform

2. Social activities

- Pony Club
- Riding clubs / Ladies groups
- Trail riding
- School holiday activities

3. Competition preparation

- Training requirements (daily, fitness)
- Coat condition (stabling, rugs, lights, clipping)
- Grooming
- Event preparation demands (days/night prior)

4. Goals

- Local / Club
- Zone
- State

5. Upskilling

- One-on-one coaching
- Horse training
- Clinics and seminars
- Demonstrations and events
- Video
- Mentor

6. Jobs with horses

- Vet
- Police
- Racing industry (stablehand/jockey/trainer)
- Riding School / Instructor / Education
- Farrier
- Nutritionist / Research
- Breeding / Horse Stud

Buying a Horse

Tips before you go out and start looking that could save you thousands of hours and dollars and increase the chances of getting a safer horse.

Horse Classifieds Decoded

Some adverts ring true but others advertised as the 16hh schoolmaster end up a 15.2hh crazy horse who can only canter one way. Jargon and sneaky phrases that appear in horse ads are enough to confuse even the most experienced of horse owners. Here's a guide to help you along your journey, and it is certainly a journey to learn by experience in the world of buying horses...

Advert Words and Phrases

•   Forward moving = Not for beginners.

•   Great on the ground = Not so good for riding.

•   Very pretty = But not so safe

•   Can be pushy = Bad manners. Will knock you over and pull you like a steam train on the ground.

•   Great trail riding horse = Not so good for anything else. Circles are not this horse's specialty.

• Cold backed = You will always have to lunge this horse before you ride it and, beware, it may still buck.

• Been to many natural horsemanship clinics = can only work with this horse on the ground and too scared to ride it.

• My horse trainer has done a lot of work with my horse = Because I'm too scared to ride it.

• Very athletic = Yes, at moving quickly underneath you.

• Would make a good all-rounder = Horse is either easy and willing to turn a hoof to most things which will be your perfect go to horse, or is not very good at anything.

• For sale with all his tack = Owner will do anything to get this crazy animal out of their sight.

• Not a novice ride = Grab the nearest pro and make sure they wear a body protector. But could be the next champion.

• Once-in-a-lifetime horse = Because your lifetime will be very short after buying the horse. OR this is an incredible horse, very special and should be selling for a good amount of money if it is a good horse and you will be lucky to have found one of these horses.

• Safe and bombproof = Good luck getting this horse to move. Great first horse for young kids and the best horse to build confidence. You are on a winner with one of these horses if you are starting out.

• Uncomplicated, easy ride = For beginners. Not a fancy horse. If you can't do basics on this horse, you need more lessons.

• Forward going and a fun ride = Doesn't come standard with brakes. Often paired with "not a novice ride" and "very athletic".

• Excellent dressage prospect = Terrible jumper, knocks all the fences. Probably has beautiful movement though.

• Very flashy = Very expensive, very good looking and a great winning competition horse with the right education.

• Can be "mareish" = The moody teenagers at your daughter's school. Can bite and kick at other horses depending on the mood. Probably try to nip you doing up the girth on the saddle.

• Started over fences = "Jumped" a cross pole twice.

• Careful jumper, never touches a pole = Will not go near a pole, thus never touches one. Or jumps much higher than necessary so hang on.

• Loose jumps 1.20m easily = Hope your paddock fences are high. Definitely talent for jumping.

• Brought on slowly/low mileage = Has done nothing even though the horse is basically old enough to vote. Probably broken in late.

• Moves beautifully = When he runs away from me as I'm trying to catch him, his extended canter looks wonderful. OR this is a very nice horse to seriously look at with the right education.

• Make an offer = If it is lower than we want (and we want too much), we will be angry. Probably had trouble selling the horse.

• Consistent jumper/dressage = Consistently below average. Or this is your awesome fun everything horse that will always try their best for you.

• Amazing bloodlines = No good for riding. Could be expensive just because of the bloodlines but might not be any good OR it could be the next winning champion.

In summary, before even going to look at a horse:

The number one piece of advice is to ask for a video to be sent to you of the horse walk, trot AND CANTER in a circle BOTH WAYS and see a nice stop. See it standing still, tied up, being groomed and having a saddle and bridle being put on. Ask your local riding school instructor who knows you to review the video and the advert so they can read between the lines and assist you with what is a good or bad option.

When you go to look at the horse, make sure the owner rides the horse first to show you what it can do because if they are too scared to ride the horse then you shouldn't get on. Don't take the excuse that they have no one to ride it for you or make sure you are comfortable after seeing the video. Maybe give it a lunge both ways first.

For beginners, stay away from forward moving – look for the words "quiet" and "no vices", older than 9yrs, preferably older than 12. 18-25yrs is absolutely fine if the horse has had regular light work and fed really well. Riding school horses have continued into their 30s.

Once a horse reaches late teens is when the price should start going down considerably based on age. As the good old saying goes: What price do you put on your children's or your own safety?

Ideally buy from a horseman or horsewoman who has grown up with horses and knows horses.

Stay away from off the track, quiet on the ground thoroughbreds unless they are older than 12 and have been well educated.

HAPPY HORSE HUNTING and GOOD LUCK WITH YOUR CHOICES

A final note

It is highly recommended to take the time to learn the basics of horse care, handling and riding preparation before stepping into the world of riding but sometimes, due to cost and time constraint, this is not achievable for most without their own horse.

Please take care in your journey to learn safely with an experienced coach and well trained horse, to ensure positive outcomes.

The information in this book is not intended or implied to be a substitute for professional medical advice, diagnosis or treatment. All content, including text, graphics, images and information, contained on or available through this book is for general information purposes only. Such information is subject to change without notice. You are encouraged to confirm any information obtained from or through this book with other sources, and review all information regarding any medical condition or treatment with your local vet or bio-security department.

UNTIL NEXT TIME... RIDE, RELAX, ENJOY

I wish you happiness and health always!

Learn more and feel better with equine energy!

LOVE, LAUGH, LIVE

DANCE AND SING

SHARE YOUR LIGHT

RUN FREE WITH HORSES

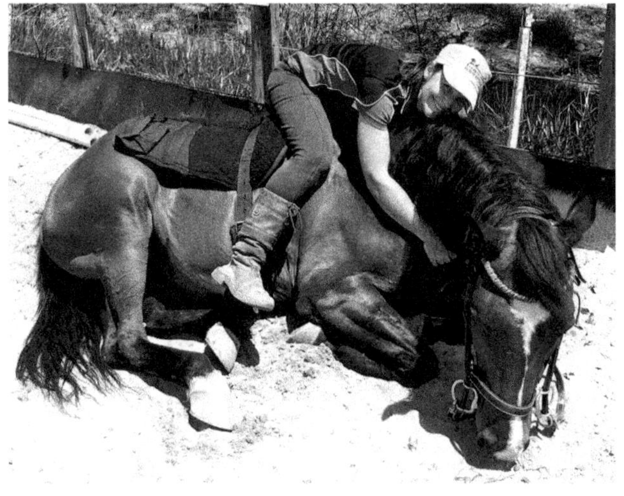

Debbie Burgermeister

Author Certifications

Equestrian Australia coach / CertIII Sports Coaching Equestrian / CertIV Trainer and Assessor / Senior First Aid, Mental Health First Aid and Blue Card / CertIV in Small Business Management / Advanced Diploma of Customer Contact Management

Further Information and Contact Details

Horse Riding Hub

info@horseridinghub.com.au

www.horseridinghub.com.au

Check out the Giddy Up Kids Programs run by Bonogin Valley Horse Retreat in Gold Coast Australia and be part of a Horse Lovers Community at *www.horseridinghub.com.au.*

GIDDY UP BEGINNER BOOKS

Collect The Series

Easy to read for kids and adults

HORSE LOVERS FIRST BOOK: A first horse book filled with colour, horse cartoons, photos and answers to the very basics you need to know about horses.

HOW TO RIDE A HORSE: Riding Lessons for Beginners Workbook as a step-by-step education resource. With a bonus development guide for parents.

READY FOR YOUR FIRST HORSE?: Read this first! An expert's guide when looking for a beginners horse for sale. Essential checklists for everything you need to find out before owning a horse.

Become A
Horse Lover Member!

Find out how at
www.horseridinghub.com/membershub

AN EDUCATION PATHWAY

Horse Lovers Worldwide

Horses are our heritage! Help keep horses a part of our community, to run free with these amazing animals. Experience the joy and freedom they bring into your life and the lives of those around you.

A resource for beginner horse lovers to obtain quality information and education for a safer horse journey.

www.ingramcontent.com/pod-product-compliance
Lightning Source LLC
LaVergne TN
LVHW080103160726
843469LV00047B/1892